FIFTY YEARS

THE NEW YORK
DAILY 🔲 NEWS

IN PICTURES

Worth Gatewood, Editor

DOUBLEDAY & COMPANY, INC.

Garden City, New York 1979

974.
7104g
Fif

Designed and produced by Duobooks Inc., New York

ISBN: 0-385-15025-3
Library of Congress Number: 78-24843

12-0293

Fifty years in Pictures had its origin in an exhibition first mounted at the Hammond Museum in North Salem, New York, in the summer of 1978 and later displayed at the New York Public Library at Fifth Avenue and 42nd Street. The pictures were selected from the thousands upon thousands of negatives on file at *The New York Daily News*, a King Solomon's Mines of newspaper photography that goes back more than half a century. The collection presented here is certainly history, but it is a good deal more than a musty archive of events long forgotten. More precisely, it is an intimate illustrated diary of the changing city and its people, a reflection of its moods, its fads and foolishness (trivia quite often mirrors an era more clearly than the record of its historians), its heroes and charlatans, and its day-to-day life. It is intended to be evocative, not definitive.

Today, news photography is taken for granted, although it is of fairly modern origin. Until Joseph Medill Patterson founded *The News* on his return from World War I service in France as an artillery captain, news photography was journalism's stepchild, considered by editors of the time to be an unnecessary evil. Patterson's idea—presenting the news in pictures with a minimum of wordage—was scorned by the conventional wisdom as unheard-of, unsound and even undignified. His pushy little paper was given six months to live. If the notion of pictorial journalism met with disapproval from other New York newspaper publishers, it was greeted with enthusiasm by the readers. In only a few years the circulation of *The News* rose to twice that of any other newspaper in America. Yet it wasn't until 1936, when *Life* magazine packaged news photography for a national audience, that Patterson's revolutionary theory won wide acceptance.

Oddly, neither the photographers who took these pictures nor their working descendants of the present have been accorded the recognition they deserve. It sometimes seems today as if *everyone* is a photographer. Galleries are crammed with the works of photographers who have won acceptance and those who hope to. Photography is discussed, dissected and analyzed in newspaper and magazine articles and in hardcover collections published in greater numbers every year. Yet the newspaper photographer and his work are seldom considered by the serious critics in the field, possibly because his efforts are held to be "non-creative." Forgotten or ignored is the fact that a first-rate news photographer requires creativity of a high order to see a picture in the fragmented scene that confronts him, to frame it in his mind and shoot it—all in a matter of seconds. He gets no second chance to record an instant of high drama and tragedy of the sort that appears on the cover of this book—the fiery destruction of the dirigible *Hindenburg* at Lakehurst, New Jersey, on May 6, 1937.

This book had its share of memorable news photographs, but it is not the intent to present a collection of dramatic pictures standing alone. Rather, the aim is to let half a century pass in review year by year, decade by decade, evoking from time to time an indulgent smile, a bittersweet memory, perhaps even a nostalgic tear from those watching in the stands. The photographs are arranged not so much by date as by the flow of events that produced them, although all but a few are presented within the frame of their decade of origin.

A format of decades was chosen because each had an almost theatrical opening and closing, with little or no part of the drama carrying over into the next. The Twenties began with Prohibition and ended in the debacle of Black Tuesday—October 29, 1929—the day the stock market crashed. The Thirties came to a belated but even more dramatic close with the thunder of Japanese bombs at Pearl Harbor. The Forties were World War II and the transition to peace and really did not end until Harry Truman left the White House. The Fifties were the placid years, although powerful forces were gathering, undetected at the time, that would change the face of the country. The Sixties dawned bright in hope and promise, with John Kennedy on hand to lead the way to some vague new Camelot. Instead, they were to be stained with turmoil, violence and bloodshed that left the country more divided than at any time since the Civil War.

More space is devoted to the Twenties because it is the decade most remote, so remote now that it is rapidly fading into myth. The Twenties were another world. Then, the nation's capital was a dull provincial city, made bearable to foreign diplomats only because it offered a nearby escape—New York. The federal government was so negligible a factor in the life of the individual that the average American's only personal contact with it was the postman who delivered his mail. President Coolidge complained that he had nothing to do, that no one ever came to see him; most afternoons, he napped. The blight of Prohibition lay upon the land, and nowhere is its futility better expressed than in the picture of the Brooklyn kids scooping up wine running down the gutters from a federal vat-smashing raid up the street. Everybody went to the movies, women to dream of being in the arms of Rudolph Valentino, men to ogle the sex symbol of the day, Clara Bow, the "It" girl; her picture is a remarkable example of changing tastes as well as times.

The Thirties shook the very foundations of the country. Pundits freely predicted bloody revolution. Newsreel audiences rose to their feet and cheered when the banker of the week was led away to prison for squandering his depositors' savings on worthless stocks; they cheered even louder when John Dillinger, Bonnie and Clyde or Pretty Boy Floyd robbed the bankers who were not already in jail. The pictures of the Great Depression reflect its grimness; the zombie-like couples shuffling across the floor in a Bronx dance marathon are a study in degradation. The country put its hope in one man, Franklin D. Roosevelt; his vigor and determination show clearly in the magnificent portrait made of him by *The News* in 1936.

In the almost total preoccupation with the drama of combat in World War II, life on the Home Front got scant attention and has been more or less neglected since. The photographs of the Forties are intended to correct the oversight. Only dimly remembered are the ration books, the scarcity of gasoline and the endless lines founded on rumors that nylons or cigarettes were available. New Yorkers accepted it all patiently and with good humor. Women came to the fore, setting such remarkable production records in war work that one wonders now why their performance was not cited as a compelling argument in the Women's Lib movement that was to emerge two decades later. We were a law-abiding lot in those days; although precious gasoline occasionally could be obtained by illegal means, the picture of Queens Boulevard eerily empty of automobiles is satisfying evidence of how honest we were.

To call the Fifties fabulous, as nostalgia hucksters have labeled the decade, is an overstatement. If anything, they were years of complacence, curiously similar to the Twenties in their self-absorption. Professors clucked in alarm at the indifference of their students to politics and public issues (only a few years later they were to be besieged in their ivory towers by howling mobs of campus radicals). But why not? Another war to end all wars had been fought. The United Nations would quickly tidy up any future international disagreements. The nation turned back to its old loves: business and a rising market. Youth was mesmerized by something called rock 'n' roll, a mixed blessing. True, there were pictures of poor blacks migrating to the cities of the North and well-off whites migrating from the cities to the suburbs, but only a perceptive few could see the powerful winds of change in those photographs.

The Sixties were a decade of mindless violence. Assassins' bullets took the lives of John F. Kennedy, Robert F. Kennedy and the Rev. Martin Luther King, Jr. Opposition to the war in Vietnam became a festering sore that erupted in bloody rioting on campuses and from there into the streets, driving a President (Lyndon B. Johnson) from office for the first time in American history. The frustrations of years boiled over in the nation's ghettos, including New York's, touching off an orgy of rioting, looting and burning that came perilously close to open rebellion. As a sort of comic relief, we had hippies, yippies and flower children whose antics seem so absurd today that one is at a loss to explain the serious attention they attracted at the time. New Yorkers suffered through a transit strike, a newspaper strike, a blackout and the world's greatest traffic jam, meanwhile playing host to visiting VIPs who ranged from Pope Paul VI to Soviet Premier Nikita Khrushchev and his Cuban branch manager, Fidel Castro. Pennsylvania Station fell to the wrecker's ball, to be replaced by the new Madison Square Garden complex. A graceful new bridge spanned the Narrows. The Mets won a World Series. The Jets won a Super Bowl. Society survived.

With a few exceptions, the photographs in this book are the work of *The New York Daily News* or its early picture-agency affiliate, Pacific & Atlantic. Credit for the others is given where known. Photographers' credit lines, seldom given by newspapers until the early Thirties, will be found at the end of the book. The striking photographs of stage, screen and television stars, originally done in color for covers of the *Sunday News Magazine*, are the work of Harry Warnecke, Bob Cranston and Gus Schoenbaechler of *The News*.

The collection was assembled with the help of Phil Greitzer of *The News* photo staff and Grover Gatewood. The photo printing was done by James Walsh of The News Photo Studio.

Not all of the faces from the past in this book called New York home, but all of them were a part of New York in their time.

—*Worth Gatewood*

THE TWENTIES

"The business of America is business."

—Calvin Coolidge, 1925

Romanticists have given the decade many labels. The Roaring Twenties.
The Jazz Age. The Era of Wonderful Nonsense. The Golden Age of Sports.
The Revolt of the Lost Generation. The years from 1920 to 1930 were all
that, certainly, but they were much more too.

In retrospect, the Twenties were the adolescent years of the nation's
emergence from its pre-World War I provincialism. They were afflicted
with the acne of social adolescence: ignorance, recklessness, mindless revolt,
frivolity, irresponsibility and vulgarity. It was a time of bathtub gin and
bootleggers, flappers and the Charleston, bobbed hair and rolled stockings,
silent movies, Mah-Jongg and radio, gangsters and tommy-guns, frenzied
stock market speculation, and the unshakable belief that prosperity would last
forever.

Yet the Twenties, tawdry as they were, produced a lasting hero,
Charles Lindbergh, and at least one benchmark on the long road to social
progress, the Nineteenth Amendment, which gave women the vote.

Sage of Baltimore

What better man to lead a pictorial parade of the
Twenties than editor, author and iconoclast H.L. Mencken,
who chronicled their follies with genial scorn.

Finis of a Phenomenon

Robed for his greatest role, "The Sheik," Rudolph Valentino was the superstar of the silent screen, idol of millions of women to whom he was the Great Lover. His death at thirty-one in New York (1926) touched off a scene of mass hysteria that neither the police nor a Fascist Blackshirt honor guard at his bier could control. Ten thousand people, mostly women, fought their way into a Broadway funeral chapel to scream, weep or faint. A hundred were injured in window-smashing pandemonium.

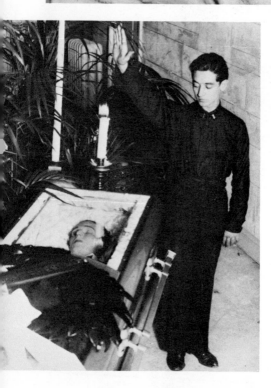

Serials, Sex and the Shimmy

Posing between the Dolly Sisters of vaudeville is bygone star
Pearl White, whose *Perils of Pauline* established her as the queen
of the movie serials—the 1920's equivalent of today's weekly
television melodramas. In those early days of the decade, the toast
of Broadway was Jeanne Eagles, star of Somerset Maugham's
then-scandalous play, *Rain,* a drama about a prostitute and a
preacher. An equally scandalous dance called the shimmy was
denounced in pulpits and papers, and the publicity made an
obscure dancer, Gilda Gray, famous overnight.

A Pair of Kings

Will Rogers, a cowboy humorist
who went on to become America's
favorite quipster and folk-philosopher,
was a rising star of a 1920s institution,
the Ziegfeld Follies. While Rogers
made the nation laugh, orchestra
leader Paul Whiteman set its toes to
tapping as the undisputed King of
Jazz. The decade was memorable for
its popular music and Whiteman
was its master. He and his wife posed
on shipboard (1923) en route to
Europe, where he was equally popular.

A Time of Talent

In a rare pose together, three of the brightest stars of the
screen—Douglas Fairbanks Sr., Mary ("America's Sweet-
heart") Pickford and Charlie Chaplin—greet the New York
ship-news photographers with an exuberance typical of the
Era of Wonderful Nonsense. Although the movies vastly
overshadowed all other entertainment in those days,
Broadway could boast of two top-flight stars of its own. One
was now-forgotten dancer Ann Pennington, whose press
agent billed her as "The Girl with the Prettiest Legs in
America." The other was unforgettable Fannie Brice, who
in 1923 prettied up her nose through cosmetic surgery
and here seems happy with her new reflection in the
dressing-room mirror.

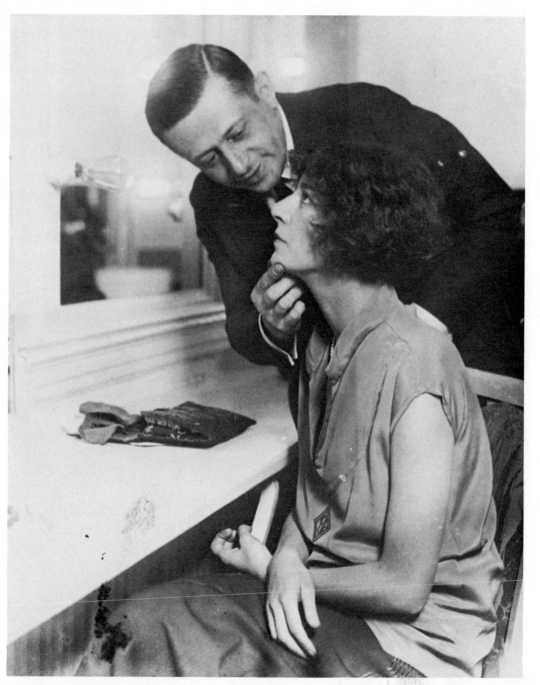

The Royal Family

The theatre was ruled by the talented, engaging and often witty Barrymores, whose domain was New York. Ethel, informed that her brother John had been driven out of his hotel and pressed into removing rubble when the San Francisco earthquake of 1906 interrupted his national tour, said, "It took an earthquake to get him out of bed and the Army to put him to work." John, known as the "Great Profile" (always the left; he would not permit his right to be photographed), was asked by a friend at the Players' Club why he was carrying on an affair with a woman twice his age when every girl in New York was throwing herself at his feet. "I think," said John, moodily, "it's because she always thanks me." Lionel, less flamboyant than his brother and sister, chose to become a character actor and not a character.

Silent Siren

Although a bit broad in the beam by today's standards, silent star Clara Bow was the fantasy of every red-blooded American male. Called the "It" girl—"It" being a Twenties euphemism for s-e-x—Clara was the first in a long line of Hollywood sex symbols that ended with star-crossed Marilyn Monroe. While Clara dominated Hollywood, a couple of New York impresarios dominated two other fields of show business—John Ringling was the circus and Florenz Ziegfeld was the famed Follies.

We Hear Voices...

When Hollywood found its voice in 1928, producers turned desperately to the New York stage for actors who could talk. One of those who went west was the distinguished and urbane Ronald Colman, whose superb diction made him an instant star. At about the same time, a new type of singing—called crooning—was being made popular by a young man who first used a megaphone and then a microphone to beguile the mass audience that radio developed. His name was Rudy Vallee and his career has spanned fifty years. In those days moviegoers worshipped goddesses; none was more venerated than the beautiful and imperious Gloria Swanson, pictured here in 1925 with her then husband, the Marquis de la Falaise.

Toast of the East: Best of the West

The darling of the New York sophisticates was uninhibited, witty and caustic stage star Tallulah Bankhead, who was to be equally admired on screen, radio and television. A story is that the imperturbable Tallulah was approached at a party one night by a young actor whose awe of the star had been overcome by drink. He told her that life would have no meaning for him if he could not share her bed, at least briefly. "You dear, old-fashioned boy," Tallulah replied. "So you shall, so you shall!" Right: Non-sophisticates west of the Hudson stood in awe of a star who scarcely said a word on screen or off. He was Tom Mix, king of the movie cowboys and idol of every small boy who could scrape up a dime for admission and a nickel for popcorn to spend Saturday morning at the movies.

Stars that Fell

The movies were not without their tragedies. Perhaps the most poignant was
that of silent screen star John Gilbert, whose untrained voice could not
meet the challenge of sound. He plummeted from fame to oblivion with the
suddenness of a snuffed-out candle. The woman by his side is his wife,
Virginia Bruce. Comedian Roscoe (Fatty) Arbuckle's career ended just as
abruptly, but for a different reason: host at a sex-and-booze party at which a
young woman died, Arbuckle was banished from the screen by the rigid
moral code of the time. On the other hand, the famous Gish sisters, Dorothy
and Lillian, were irreproachable both off screen and on. Their pictures
could be summed up in a word: wholesome.

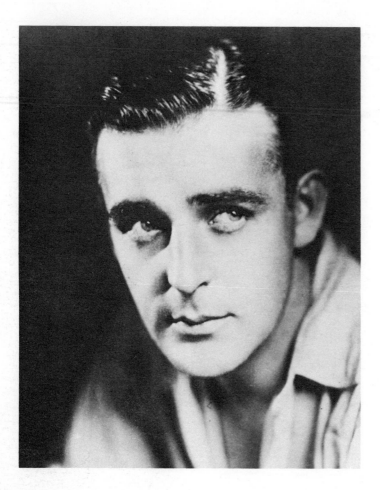

Sinner and Savior

Now almost totally forgotten, Wallace Reid ranked second only to Valentino as a matinee idol. Addicted to alcohol and narcotics, Reid died at the peak of his career, precipitating a drug scandal that shook Hollywood and its New York financiers to their foundations and led the more strident moralists to demand that movies be banned as a threat to public decency. Among those who helped the screen refurbish its tarnished image were straight-arrow funnyman Harold Lloyd and his leading lady, Mildred Davis. Their pictures were comedic morality plays. Lloyd was a rarity—a strictly business star who wisely invested his money and became a millionaire many times over.

A Pride of Literary Lions

Crass as the Twenties were, they produced three of America's finest writers. In *The Sun Also Rises*, the young Ernest Hemingway had been recognized as the spokesman for the disillusioned Lost Generation, and was working on *A Farewell to Arms*. He and his wife had just arrived from Europe. F. Scott Fitzgerald had just finished his memorable *Great Gatsby* and was vacationing in France with his beloved daughter, "Scottie."

The Playwright Cometh

The third of the triumvirate, Sinclair Lewis, first American to win the Nobel Prize for Literature, had established his reputation with satiric novels on American life, *Main Street* (1920) and *Babbitt* (1922). The Twenties also saw the emergence of America's greatest playwright, Eugene O'Neill. At this point O'Neill had established his commanding talent with *The Emperor Jones* and *Anna Christie*.

Twilight of the Tycoons

The age of the financial tycoon was drawing to an end, but the piratical J. Pierpont Morgan remained the archetypical capitalist. Morgan lived as a man of his importance was expected to live—baronially—in this New York townhouse. What Morgan didn't control, the aging John D. Rockefeller, Sr. did. Here he is seen in his annual birthday ritual: presenting a small boy with a nickel, an idea said to have been suggested by press agent Ivy Lee to improve his image. John D. later upped his largesse to a dime.

Low Finance

A financier of a different kind, Charles Ponzi gave his name to a classic stock swindle in which early investors are paid off with money supplied by later ones. On hand too, to siphon off the easy money of the Twenties, were the gangsters. Spawned by Prohibition, they supplied thirsty New Yorkers with beer and bathtub gin and killed each other in incessant wars over the profits. This one is dapper, moustached Vincent ("Mad Dog") Coll.

Prelude to the Godfather

The most celebrated New York gangster of the time was natty Jack ("Legs") Diamond, who survived so many bullets he was known as the human clay pigeon. But he too met his end at the hands of competitors in 1931 and became the subject of a standard photo of the time: mourning widow at bier of slain husband. If you feel that movie portrayals of gangland funerals are overdrawn, consider: on the last ride of Frankie Yale through Brooklyn, 250 cars—38 of them carrying flowers—followed the hearse containing his $15,000 silver coffin. The attendance was estimated at 15,000, including his *two* widows.

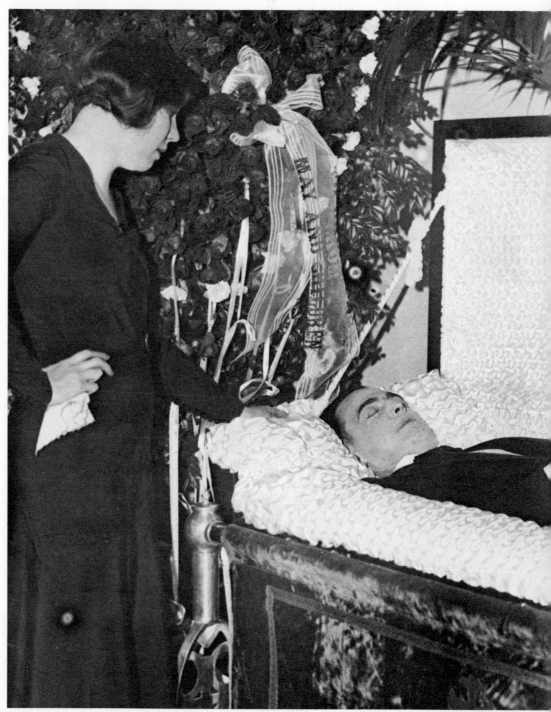

The Passionate Preacher

The crime of the decade was the murder, still unsolved, of the
Rev. Edward Hall and Mrs. James Mills. The philandering pastor
and the comely choir singer, involved in what was then called an illicit
romance, were shot to death—together—in romantically named
DeRussey's Lane in New Jersey. The forbidding Gothic home of the
Rev. Hall in New Brunswick, New Jersey, drew curiosity-seekers
for years as the case wore along through two trials. Inflicting
the punishment for murder was the job of cadaverous Robert Elliott.
He was New York State's official executioner. Among his victims was
Ruth Snyder who, with her lover Judd Gray, was convicted of bashing
her husband to death with a sashweight. This picture of Snyder
dying in the electric chair at Sing Sing Prison aroused a storm of
controversy, focused public attention on capital punishment and
likely was a factor in its virtual abolition over the years.

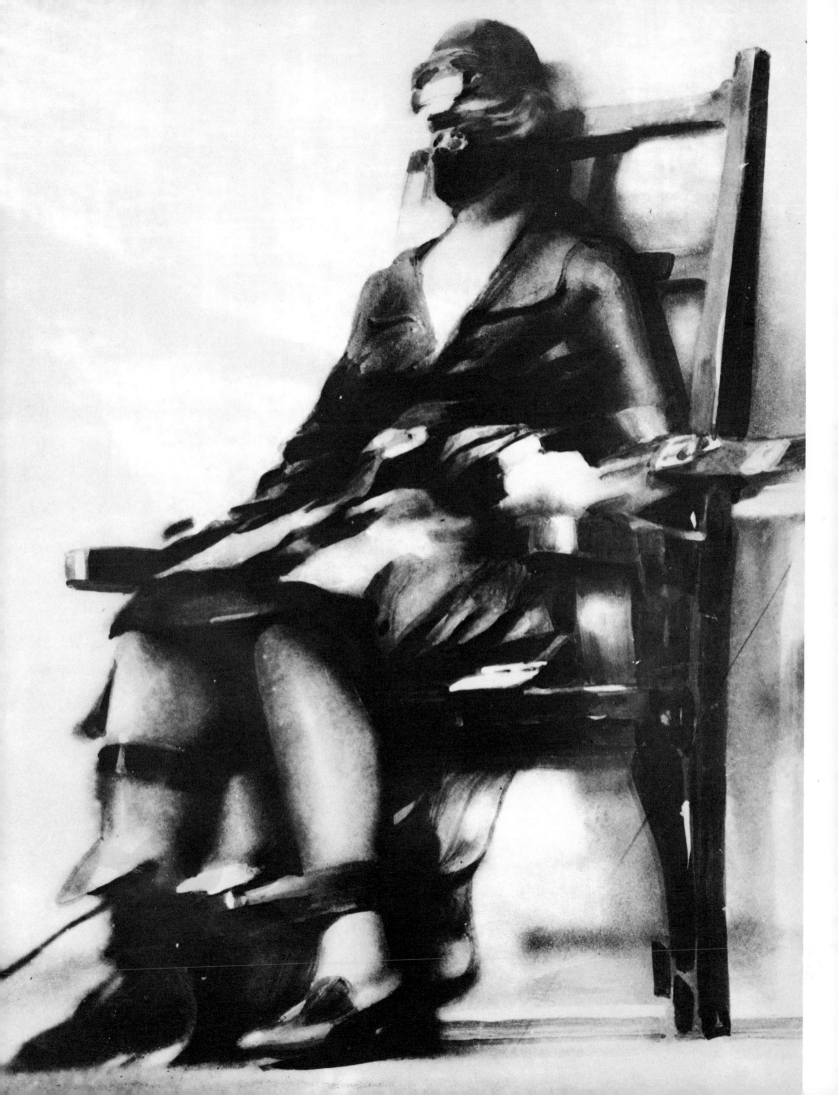

Silent Cal, Jaunty Jimmy

Presiding over most of the decade was dour
Calvin Coolidge, a man of few words and even fewer
expressed ideas. So taciturn was he that a visitor,
desperately seeking a conversational opener,
wondered aloud if the rain that had been falling all
day would ever stop. "It always has," replied
Coolidge, lapsing again into silence. A totally different
type—Mayor James J. Walker—presided over
New York City. Dapper, flamboyant, charming,
persuasive, witty, frequently frivolous and often
irresponsible, Walker was suited to his time.
Everybody loved him except the reformers. They
brought him down in disgrace. In the historic
photograph at right are a President, three Governors
of New York and a Senator: Franklin D. Roosevelt,
President and Governor; Herbert H. Lehman,
Governor and Senator; and Alfred E. Smith, Governor.

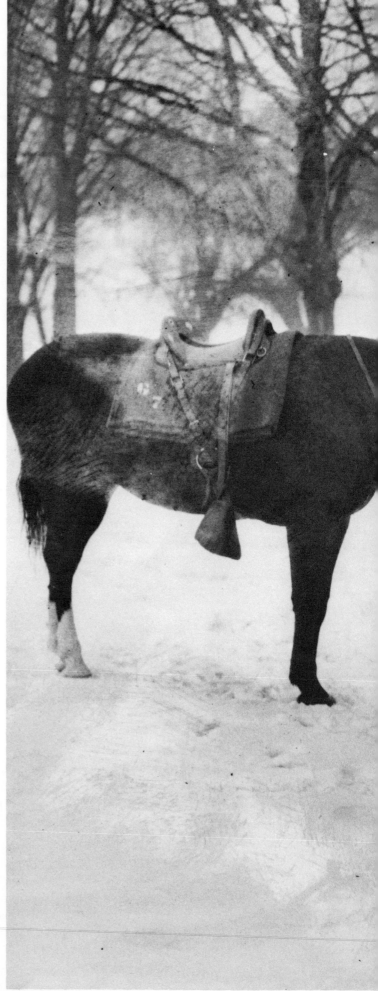

A Wet and the Drys

Here is the more familiar Al Smith, with derby and cigar, shown with his wife. He ran for President in 1928, but his Catholicism and blunt opposition to Prohibition were hurdles he could not overcome. Smith predicted Prohibition would spawn lawlessness. It did. In one of the first futile attempts to enforce the new law the New York State Constabulary frisks the occupants of a halted car for bootleg booze.

Overleaf: The feds couldn't win for losing. While they smashed illegal wine vats up the street in Brooklyn, the kids down the block scooped up the wine from the gutters and ran home with it.

Bootleg Boutique

This modishly attired lady is demonstrating the cane flask, a wily means of evading the Prohibition snoopers. Filled with bathtub gin, it quenched the thirst and served as a steadying prop when empty. Supplying such law-evaders were the rum runners who met the booze ships coming up from Bermuda or wherever, transferred the cargo and ran it ashore in the dead of night. These boats ran afoul of the Coast Guard and were impounded at Port Newark.

Titans of the Twenties

Truly a Golden Age of Sports, the Twenties produced some enduring heroes. The most enduring is the Yankees' "Sultan of Swat," the legendary Babe Ruth, here in his prime in 1924. Then there was the equally legendary Frankie Frisch, the "Fordham Flash," third baseman for the Giants in 1921. Sharing the fame of their teams were the two most powerful managers of the day: the Yankees' Miller Huggins and the Giants' John McGraw. Perhaps the most dazzling baseball infield of the Twenties was that of the champion 1928 Yankees: Leo Durocher, Lou Gehrig, Tony Lazzeri, Joe Dugan, Pat Collins, Gene Robertson and Mark Koenig.

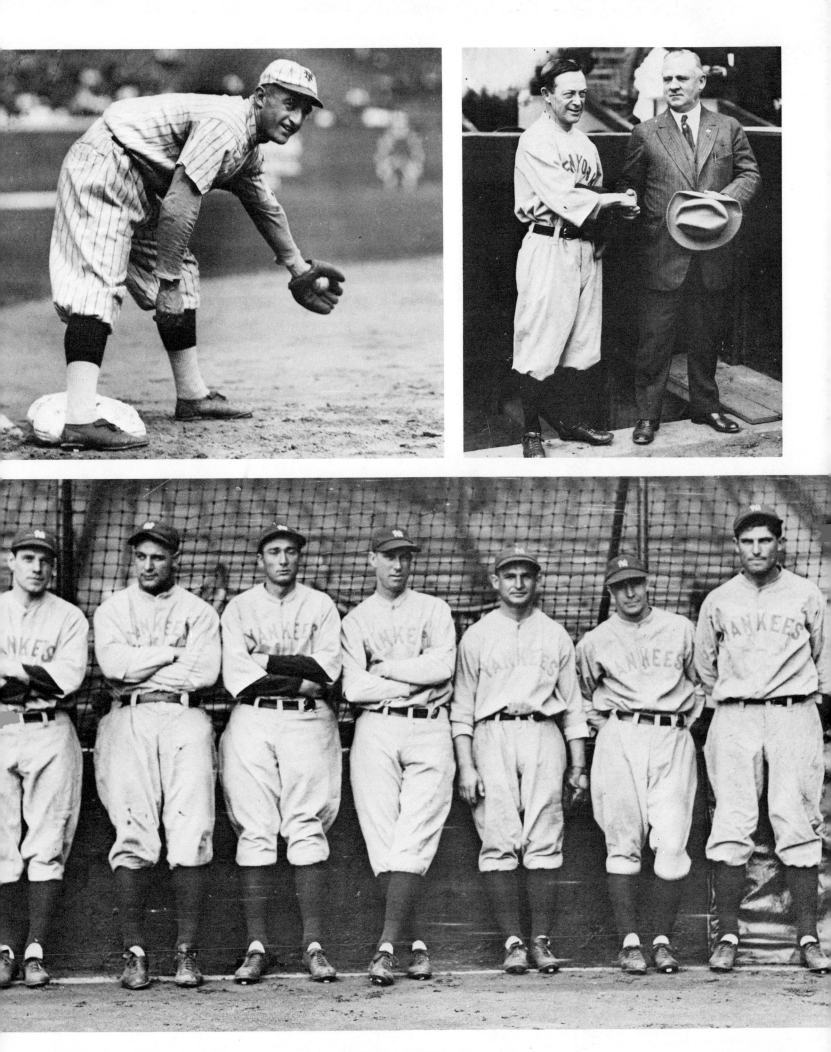

...And Still the Champ

Of all modern-day heavyweight champions, Jack Dempsey was the most popular. And still is. Knocked out of the ring by Luis Firpo at Madison Square Garden in 1923 in the first round of the decade's most exciting fight, Dempsey climbed back in and flattened Firpo in the next. Likened to a tiger in the ring, Dempsey fought, rather than boxed, with frightening ferocity. Even posing in his black tights he seemed menacing. But in 1926 he met a better boxer, a young ex-Marine of World War I named Gene Tunney, and lost his title. Out of the ring, Dempsey was an easy-going charmer who, after the fashion of fighters of his time, courted movie actresses and married one— Estelle Taylor.

Our Heroine

In 1926, New York's own Gertrude Ederle became the first woman to swim the icy English Channel, crossing it in a record 14 hours and 31 minutes, aided only by a thick coat of grease to protect her from the cold. Her feat created a sensation and her popularity rivaled that of football immortal Harold ("Red") Grange, the Galloping Ghost of the University of Illinois. In the early days of pro football, Grange filled the stands when he played at the old Polo Grounds.

The Boys of Autumn

Although the Notre Dame campus lies in distant South Bend, Indiana, the biggest and fiercest band of Fighting Irish fans—the famed "subway alumni"—were and are in New York. Their hero in the Twenties was famed coach Knute Rockne. He had the best backfield in the land: Harry Stuhldreher, Elmer Layden, James Crowley and Donald Miller, dubbed the "Four Horsemen" by sportswriter Grantland Rice. Biggest game of the year in New York was Army vs. Notre Dame. Notre Dame won the 1928 classic, 12-6. The player catching the pass was Army's great Chris Cagle.

60

A Galaxy of Greats

If America seemed obsessed with sports in the Twenties, there was a reason: the decade produced dazzling champions, names that are as familiar now as they were fifty years ago. In track, long-distance runner Paavo Nurmi, the "Flying Finn," set twenty world records and won six Olympic titles from 1920 to 1932. Still talked of today are three golfers: Walter Hagen, Bobby Jones and Gene Sarazen. Hagen won the U.S. Open twice, the British Open four times and the PGA five times. Jones won the U.S. Open three times, the National Amateur four times and the British Open twice. In 1930 he stroked a grand slam: U.S. Open, National Amateur, British Open, British Amateur. Sarazen, once a caddy at Rye, won the U.S. Open twice (the first time when he was only twenty), the British Open once and the PGA three times. In tennis, two players stood above all others —William ("Big Bill") Tilden and Helen Wills Moody. Some say they were the best ever. Tilden won the U.S. Singles seven times, the Professional Singles twice and the British Singles three times. At fifty-two, with Vinnie Richards, he won the Professional Doubles. Moody won the U.S. Women's Singles seven times, the British Singles five times. Forest Hills was their showcase. At Belmont Park, the crowds rooted home the leading jockey of the day, Earl Sande, shown here aboard Zev, winner of the 1923 Kentucky Derby.

The Decade's Darker Side

Although we think of the Twenties as a time of flappers, flasks and frivolity, it had its grim side. The stark photo below reminds us that terrorist bombings are no recent malignancy in our society. On September 16, 1920, a time-bomb exploded in a horse-drawn wagon on Wall Street, killing thirty and injuring scores. The case was never solved. And in one of the most dramatic photos ever taken, terrified passengers hang on for life as the *S.S. Vestris* heels over on her way to the bottom of the Atlantic off the Virginia Capes in 1928. Bound for Argentina, the *Vestris* foundered in a storm two days out of New York. Fortunately, most of her 328 passengers and crew were rescued. A crewman took this picture with an $8.50 camera and sold it to *The News* for $1,500.

Overleaf: One of the first, if not the first, air views of New York, 1924.

We Were Snarling About Traffic Even Then

In 1923, New York City's arteries were as clogged as they are today and
there were the same demands that somebody should do something about it.
Nobody ever has. At left, Times Square. Note that the trolleys, like
today's buses, traveled in threes. Fifth Avenue was then the domain of the
double-decker bus, beloved of tourists who considered the splendors of
the avenue well worth exposure to soot and cinders.

A Grace Note

Now only a decaying reminder of a more gracious age, the city's bustling transatlantic piers were once its pride. Then, the stately Woolworth Building proudly dominated the lower Manhattan skyline. Now it is lost in the shadows of newer, taller, but far less elegant buildings.

Supermarket, 1924

The pushcart peddlers along Rivington Street not only sold everything, they *knew* everything. Shopping was as much recreation as necessity, an opportunity to gossip and gawk. But the teeming Lower East Side was a part of New York seldom seen by VIPs welcomed to New York by the city's official greeter, Grover Whalen. Always dressed to the nines, he met the ships, presented the keys to the city to visiting celebrities and led parades, which is what he is doing here.

Echo of the Past

In a poignant bit of history, three-time presidential candidate William Jennings Bryan, most noted orator of his day, hears his final political hurrah at the 1924 Democratic National Convention at the old Madison Square Garden.

The Thigh Was the Limit

Swim suits were becoming shockingly scanty in 1925, as the coy lass in white with hand on hip demonstrates in a pose with ladies modeling beach wear of earlier years. Even more shocking to the older generation was a hoisted-skirt dance called the Charleston, in which a girl sometimes dared to bare a flash of thigh. Everybody was doing the Charleston, including these nine girls who were brought to New York to compete in a national dance-off. They rehearsed on the roof of the old Hotel McAlpin. For the untalented girl who couldn't do anything except just look pretty, there was the newly contrived bathing beauty contest that had emerged in Atlantic City. The prizes were paltry. About all a winner could be assured of was getting her picture in the paper. The knickers worn by the judges in the foreground were called "plus-fours" and were the last word in sartorial splendor for the debonair.

Bait for Big Spenders

A curious phenomenon of the Twenties, Texas Guinan was front-woman and hostess for a number of mob-run night clubs in New York's Prohibition era. Brash, tough-talking but honest, her standard greeting to the customers was "Hello, sucker!" Like Toots Shor in later years, she became a celebrity in her own right. Here she poses in 1928 with her "girls," who sang and danced after a fashion but whose primary duty was to keep the cash flowing from the big "butter-and-egg-men," as heavy spenders were called in those days.

The Voyage Was Bon

"Like all good New Yorkers, we went to Europe every year." So said Gertrude Stein. Some of the "good New Yorkers" chose to cross on the only major U.S. competitor on the Atlantic run, the *Leviathan*, shown here outward bound for England. What the lumbering *Leviathan* lacked in speed she made up for in elegance and service; in her first-class dining salon black-tie was de rigueur and there seemed to be a waiter for every table. But the "beautiful people" of the time preferred to sail on Britain's *Mauretania*, whose passenger list on every crossing was a celebrity index for both sides of the Atlantic.

Hokum...and a Hero

Every generation has its peddlers of self-improvement nostrums. They vary only in degree of quackery. In the Twenties it was a Frenchman, Dr. Emile Coué, who was all the rage. His magic was simple. All one had to do was say aloud and at frequent intervals: "Every day in every way I am getting better and better." But Dr. Coué was quickly forgotten in the never-equaled tumult that greeted Charles A. Lindbergh's historic solo flight from New York to Paris in 33 hours, 29 minutes and 30 seconds. The busy city came to a standstill as all New York took to the streets to welcome home the decade's only authentic hero.

The Day the Bubble Burst

Muscular, hell-roaring evangelist Billy Sunday, the Billy Graham of his day, warned the profligates that the end was coming. It came—on October 29, 1929—forever to be known as Black Tuesday—when the stock market, swollen by years of reckless gambling, collapsed with a crash heard 'round the world. The loss was to be $50 billion. The party was over and it was time to pay the piper.

THE THIRTIES

"The only thing we have to fear is fear itself."

—Franklin D. Roosevelt, 1933

A bleak period in American history, the Thirties are best described by the title of Edward Robb Ellis's fine book on those terrible times, *A Nation in Torment.*

Sixteen million people—one third of the nation's working force—were jobless. A million and a half or perhaps even two million of them roamed the country, hitchhiking or riding freight trains, vainly looking for work of any kind, anywhere.

Banks failed every day, 1,326 of them in one year alone, 1930. The gross national product fell from $103 billion to $55 billion. Mills and factories closed their gates. Half-built skyscrapers were abandoned to rust. The song of the day was a lament, "Brother, Can You Spare a Dime?"

Worse still was a crisis of faith. America's leaders—politicians, economists, businessmen and bankers—had promised a "permanent plateau of prosperity." They had proved to be fools or charlatans. Bankers in particular felt the whip of the public scorn. "The bastards broke the people's back with their usury!" angrily shouted New York's Congressman Fiorello LaGuardia. Will Rogers told his readers how to determine if a banker had a glass eye: "It's the one with the glint of human kindness in it."

The nation wondered to whom it could turn.

The New Dealer

It turned to Franklin D. Roosevelt. No President since Lincoln so
dominated his time. Leader of a bloodless revolution, Roosevelt—for the
first time in the nation's history—applied the resources of the federal
government directly to the welfare of the people. Here is FDR at the peak
of his power and vigor in 1936.

The Great Depression

Trapped in the past, President Herbert Hoover seemed to suffer a paralysis of the will in the face of the gathering storm. In New York, hundreds of World War I veterans crowded into buses to join the Bonus March on Washington in 1932. Hoover refused to hear their pleas. Instead, he ordered troops under Gen. Douglas MacArthur to disband the veterans. Troopers drove them out of their shacks with billies and sabers. The ex-doughboys from New York came home, some with broken heads, all with broken hopes.

THIS TOKEN EXPIRES DECEMBER 31, 1933

$1 MUTUAL EXCHANGE SYSTEM $1

TOKEN

ONE DOLLAR TOKEN

This represents a credit of One Dollar
in goods or services to be produced and or supplied by the active
membership to the bearer when available by or through

PRESIDENT   MANAGER

Acceptance of this token makes the user a supporting
member of the Mutual Exchange System, but involves
no responsibility by him on behalf of the organization.

The goods and or services called for by this token are to be supplied only by active members

ONE DOLLAR TOKEN

When the Banks Closed

Scrip, issued locally and called "funny money," filled the gap
when President Roosevelt closed the country's 19,000 banks
for three days in 1933. Thousands of banks had already failed.
The biggest single bank failure was that of the Bank of the
United States in New York. It shut its doors in 1930, wiping out
500,000 depositors. There was no FDIC then to protect them
from loss. Jobless, homeless and hungry, 10,500 men went through
this breadline in one day at the city's Municipal Lodging House.

Subways Were for Sleeping

Wrapped in newspapers, with packing boxes to ward off the cold, thousands of homeless turned the miles of underground corridors into dormitories each night. The overflow made do in shantytowns—derisively called "Hoovervilles"—or in abandoned construction foundations. This one was home for a dozen men at 42nd Street and the East River, where the United Nations now stands.

Homeless, Hopeless

The more ambitious unemployed sometimes built rather elaborate shelters from what lay at hand: bricks, tin, discarded lumber. This one, almost manorial for the times, graced the "Hooverville" in the lower reservoir area of Central Park in 1932. An individualist, this woman preferred the privacy of her own packing box. Her address? Park Place. A *News* reporter, Todd Wright, was assigned to join the apple sellers who stood on the streets in 1931 in a pitiable effort to become self-supporting. Wright found the experience humiliating for buyer and seller.

Hamburgers, 5 Cents

One of the first of Roosevelt's many moves to revitalize the economy was the NRA—the National Recovery Administration, whose symbol was the Blue Eagle and whose motto was "We Do Our Part." A voluntary program to establish fair prices and wages, the NRA set a minimum wage of $14.50—a week, not a day. The theme song of FDR's New Deal was "Happy Days Are Here Again." They weren't, really, but they were at least happier than they had been a year earlier. This good-natured crowd was collecting its pay from a government project called the WPA—Works Progress Administration. The pay? It averaged $45 a month. Old Man Prohibition hung in effigy from a flagpole as New York celebrated the advent of Repeal in 1933 after thirteen years of bootleg booze. For a sign of the times, note the price of hamburgers on the corner restaurant.

The Return of Demon Rum

A celebrant who gave his name as Herbert Chase won immortality
of a sort: he was the first drunk arrested after Repeal. While
Mr. Chase slept it off in the slammer, the girls at the old Hollywood
Club drank a toast backstage to the death of Prohibition.

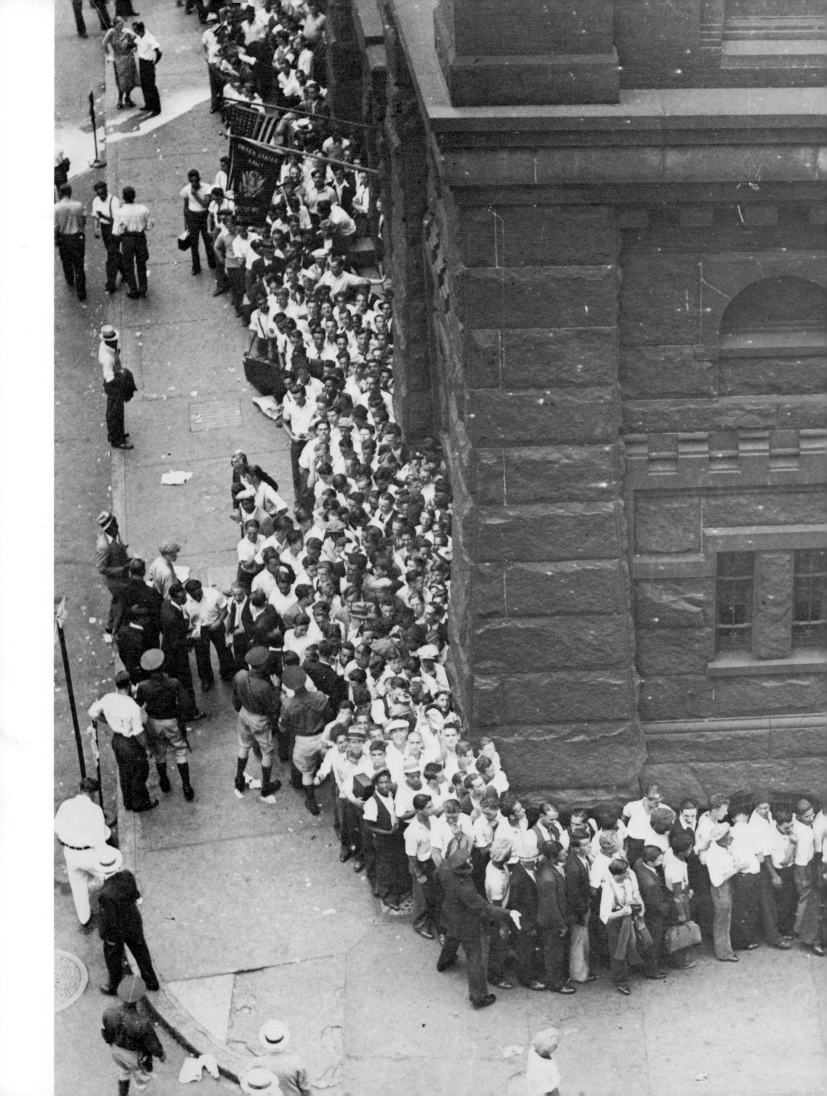

The Tree Army

The young men lined up in 1933 at Army Headquarters downtown were enlisting in the Civilian Conservation Corps, the one Roosevelt innovation that won universal praise. At its peak in 1935, the CCC took 500,000 men from 18 to 25 off the streets and freight trains and put them to work planting trees, clearing firebreaks and building roads. In the nine years of its existence the CCC planted *one billion* trees. The pay was $30 a month, $25 of which was sent directly to the enlistee's family. He got the remaining $5.

Hope Was Building

Despite the times, the spirit of the city never flagged. It found expression in cable, steel, stone and concrete. The handsome George Washington Bridge gracefully spanned the Hudson River in 1931 and was in its final stage of construction. A year later, Rockefeller Center was thrusting itself to dominance over mid-Manhattan. And some saw in the gleamingly new Empire State Building a soaring symbol of better times to come.

Times Square, 1932

The heart of the city beat in Times Square, as yet unstained by pornography, prostitution and predators.

The Little Flower

Fiorello ("The Little Flower") LaGuardia not only was Mayor of New York, he *was* New York. He ran everything, and ran it efficiently. Not a limousine type, LaGuardia raced around town in the side car of a police motorcycle, fighting fires, quelling riots and unsnarling traffic jams. On the East Side, reigning debutante Brenda Frazier and her white-tied escorts graced the Velvet Ball at the Waldorf . . . in the Bronx, exhausted couples, asleep on their feet, shuffled around the floor in one of the most degrading spectacles of the Thirties—the marathon dance. More often than not, the promoter decamped with the paltry prize money.

Infamous and the Famous

This composed and not-unhandsome man was the perpetrator of what the press called the crime of the century—the kidnap-murder of the Lindbergh baby. His name was Bruno Richard Hauptmann and he died in the electric chair in Trenton, New Jersey, in 1935. But crime occupied little space in the newspapers of the day. Rather, the public wanted heroes. One was the most noted woman pilot of her day, Amelia Earhart, a frequent New York visitor. She and her co-pilot were lost on a mysterious flight over the Pacific in 1937. Douglas ("Wrong-Way") Corrigan struck a lighter note in aviation. Landing in Dublin in 1938 after an impromptu solo flight from New York, without clearance or papers, Corrigan asked where he was. "Dublin?" he repeated. "That's funny. I thought I was in Los Angeles. I must have flown the wrong way."

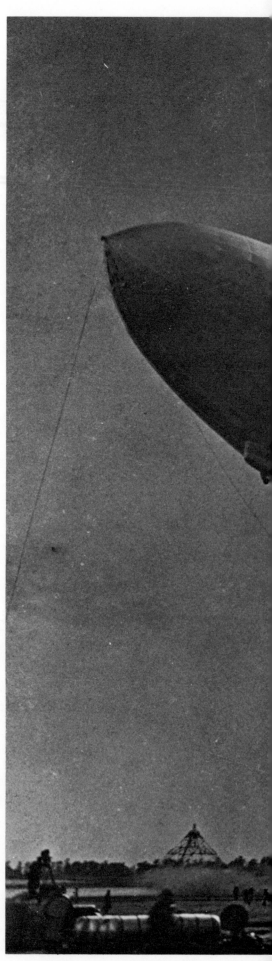

Disasters by Fire

The passenger-carrying dirigible *Hindenburg* cruises over Long Island Sound on her regular flight from Germany. A fiery end awaited her on that day, May 6, 1937, when in a spring thunderstorm her hydrogen lifting gas ignited as she was being moored at Lakehurst, New Jersey. The disaster took thirty-six lives. A victim of fire at sea in 1934, the smoldering hulk of the *Morro Castle* lies just off the beach at Asbury Park, New Jersey. The disaster, which took 125 lives, raised ugly hints of arson, mutiny and even murder and remains an unsolved mystery.

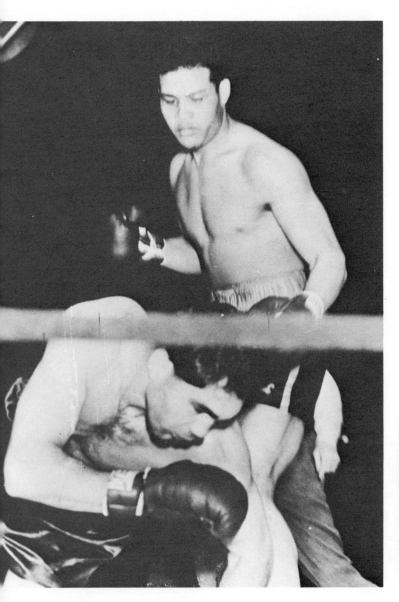

Championship Form

The Yankees in the 1930s, as usual, had their superstar: Joe DiMaggio, now a superstar of television commercials. The heavyweight fight of the decade was Joe ("The Brown Bomber") Louis's one-round destruction of Hitler's Aryan pride, Max Schmeling, at Madison Square Garden in 1938. It took 2,000 police, plus fire hoses, to keep 100,000 celebrants under control in Harlem. The incredible Babe Didrikson dominated women's sports. She excelled in basketball, baseball and track, winning two Olympic events in the latter, and took fifty tournament titles in golf.

At the Movies

The screen beauty of her time, Jean Harlow was the original Platinum Blonde, inheritress of Clara Bow's role as sex symbol. Her pressured career and tragic death at only twenty-six in 1937 was to have a curious parallel to that of the girl who followed in her fame, Marilyn Monroe. More serious film-followers had taken note of a young actress named Bette Davis, whose role in *Of Human Bondage* in 1934 set her on the way to becoming a dramatic actress of the first rank. *It Happened One Night*, starring Clark Gable and Claudette Colbert, swept the Oscars in 1934: Best Actor, Best Actress, Best Picture. The movie established Gable as king of the box office, a title he held until his death in 1960.

The Way They Looked...

Forty years ago, these famous stars were rising on the horizon of show business. *The New York Daily News* took note of their promise by printing their pictures in color on the cover of its Sunday Magazine. How many of them can you identify today? If memory fails, read on from the left: Joan Crawford. Fred Astaire and Ginger Rogers. Lena Horne. Bob Hope and Dorothy Lamour. Bing Crosby. Katharine Hepburn. Jimmy Stewart. Carole Lombard. Shirley Temple. W. C. Fields.

End Piece

The author of the Thirties was John Steinbeck, whose greatest novel,
The Grapes of Wrath, was the decade's most compelling social document.
Its pitiless look at a collapsing society was in a measure responsible for
the social legislation that corrected the inequities of the times. The decade
ended with a gala party given in 1939 by New York for the world. It was
called the World's Fair and its Perisphere and Trylon were, it was hoped,
symbols of progress through peace. The hope was soon dashed.

THE FORTIES

"Praise the Lord and pass the ammunition!"

—Navy chaplain Howell Forgy, during the attack on Pearl Harbor

The Forties were The War. On December 7, 1941, life in New York, as elsewhere in the country, changed with jolting suddenness. Drift was replaced by a challenging goal: defeat Japan and Germany! The task came to be known as the War Effort. It was to be a stupendous achievement of production, one too little remembered today.

Consider: fighting a two-hemisphere war with more than sixteen million men and women under arms, the United States, at the same time, supplied its Allies with the bulk of their needs and maintained a more-than-adequate economy at home. Even more remarkable, inflation was never a factor.

On the Home Front there were shortages of this and that, disruptions and dislocations, but no real hardship. New words and phrases came into the language: rationing, the Black Market, OPA (Office of Price Administration), V-Mail, the Dear John Letter, Rosie the Riveter, Meatless Tuesday. People sang a sentimental song, "You Are My Sunshine," and a silly one, "Mairzy Doats."

As the port of embarkation and supply center for Europe, New York was closer to the war than any other mainland city except San Francisco. Its reputation for hospitality to those in uniform was legendary. "Even if you got money, they won't let you spend it," said an overwhelmed soldier.

New York did its part.

The Man from Missouri

Although Roosevelt was at the nation's helm into 1945, the decade rightly belongs to President Harry Truman, whose lonely decision it was to trigger the atomic bomb over Hiroshima and later to boldly defy a Soviet blockade with the Berlin Airlift. Derided as a political accident and unfairly compared to his illustrious predecessor, Truman went on to become one of the most unwavering men ever to occupy the White House. No one at the time saw the significance of that no-nonsense mouth and determined chin.

The Bugle Calls

The decade began ominously with the nation's first peacetime draft in 1940. Visibly moved by the seriousness of the occasion, President Roosevelt watched while blindfolded Attorney General Robert Jackson drew one of the first numbers in Washington. The "winners" in New York accepted the draft with no protests, no riots, not even any long faces. They took it as a lark, laughingly ready for whatever lay in store for them at Fort Dix. What lay in store was the mess sergeant's order to swab down the chow hall. Nobody had ever heard the word ambiance in those days, but the chow hall was very short on it.

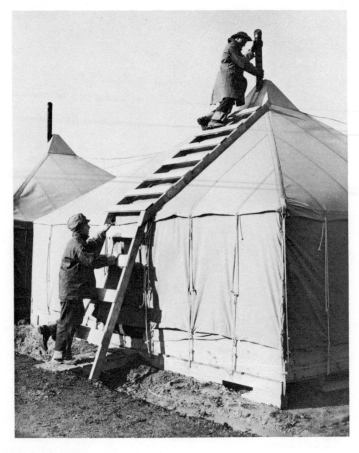

$21 a Day—Once a Month

Home was the pyramidal tent, hot in summer, cold
in winter, clammy in rain and, somehow, surrounded
by mud in any weather. Few today realize that the
armed services were segregated in World War II.
This is the 369th Coast Artillery, Harlem's own
National Guard outfit, being mustered into federal
service months before Pearl Harbor.

An Inglorious End

The city's most dramatic casualty of the war was a ship—the *Normandie*, glory of the French line and the favorite of traveling New Yorkers in the last years of peace. Caught in New York by the outbreak of the war in Europe in 1939, the *Normandie* remained at her pier. Early in 1942 a fire broke out aboard and soon raged out of control. Made topheavy by the thousands of tons of water poured into her by fireboats, the *Normandie* began to list . . . then rolled over and sank at her dock, an inglorious end for so splendid a ship.

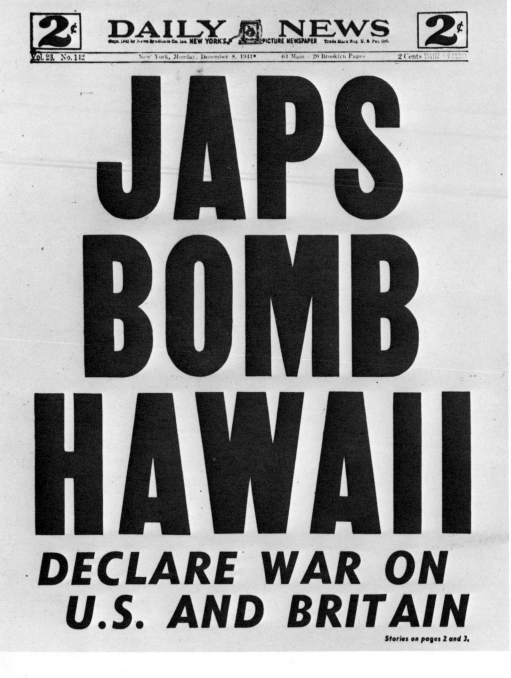

A Day of Infamy

On the morning of December 8, 1941, there was only one story. No one dreamed then of how drastically the war would change their lives. Life as America had known it was never to return. Although New York City was in no danger, the Empire State Building was experimentally blacked out on the night of December 9. Only two tiny lights (top center of large picture) betrayed its presence. But a dimout was ordered for the duration. Street lights were painted black on top so that they would be less visible from above. A workman here is installing a wartime light on East 42nd Street, with the Third Avenue El in the background.

Home Front Hassle

Then came rationing, so many points for this, so many points for that. There were endless lines for a War Ration Book and endless forms to fill out. New Yorkers took it good humoredly and passed the hours exchanging tips on what store was rumored to have what scarce article for sale. The ration book with its cryptic letters and numbers was so precious that its owner would surrender his money to a robber but risk his life for the book.

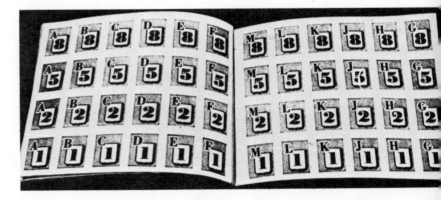

Gas Pains

Gasoline was precious, too. A motorist saw this tank truck and, surmising that it was heading for a filling station, pulled in behind. Other drivers pulled in behind him. When the truck driver arrived at the filling station he was leading a parade. Trimly uniformed girls began to handle the gas pumps as the draft drained away the young men. The price on the pump, 22 cents, is enough to induce acute nostalgia. The lady in the limo was in bad trouble. The OPA inspector confiscated her gas ration book for joyriding, which was strictly forbidden. She said she was going to a cemetery. He said she was going to a theater. She lost her book and with it her wheels.

Overleaf: Arbitrary and sometimes officious it might have been, but gas rationing worked. The proof is this empty stretch of Queens Boulevard looking toward the city from Forest Hills.

Blue Collar Belles

The war required previously undreamed-of levels of production in everything from screws to ships. But where to get the manpower? The answer was womanpower. Women handled dirty and dangerous jobs with skill and without complaint, setting production records and sticking to their machines with far less absenteeism than the men they had supplanted. Others did volunteer work for the Red Cross. These women packed food parcels for our prisoners of war in Japan and Germany.

Role Call

The Women's Army Corps beckoned to many who wanted an active part
in the war. These two WACs modeled the new uniform that helped
spur recruiting. Those with the figure and talent for it displayed both in
boosting the morale of Our Boys. Our Boys were appreciative. These
high-kicking morale boosters were the Gae Foster Girls, doing their bit for
the USO in Central Park Mall. If you wanted to forget the war briefly,
you could always relax with the latest gossip about three of the in-women of
the times: Woolworth heiress Barbara Hutton, the lady in black; smiling
model Sabina, the Farrah Fawcett-Majors of her time; and leopard-jacketed
multimillionairess Doris Duke, who was around town with her friend,
Honeychild Wilder.

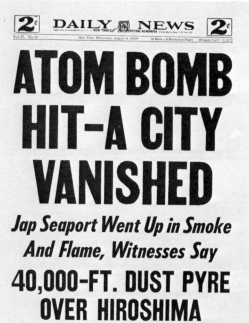

An End and a Beginning

The death in 1945 of its favorite son, President Roosevelt, stunned the city. New York paused in prayer but went on with its work of winning the war. But work was forgotten on V-E Day in May 1945 when the city threw a party as only New York knows how. It began in Times Square and became a movable feast. Some of the celebrants didn't get home for days. Then, with the suddenness of a thunderclap, the world's first atomic bomb ended the war with Japan in August 1945.

Over Here

On her first post-war trip to New York, the *Queen Mary* carried only one class: happy. These were the first troops home from Europe. The city broke out the flags and the drinks. Not long after came the war brides from England and France, a bit apprehensive about the strange new world they faced. New York made them welcome, too.

Overleaf: The war wasn't officially over for New York until it had hosted a Victory Parade, starring the Army's elite 82nd Airborne Division. Here the troopers step off under the Washington Arch for a four-mile march up Fifth Avenue.

Nightmare on 34th Street

In an accident so improbable as to be almost beyond belief, a fog-blinded Army B-25 bomber crashed into the Empire State Building between the seventy-eighth and seventy-ninth floors. Its speed carried the bomber entirely through the wall, spewing wreckage and fire into the seventy-ninth floor and turning the offices of the Catholic War Relief Services into an inferno. The tragedy occurred on July 28, 1945, and took thirteen lives.

The Swoon Set

Until the late Forties, teenagers had never been
accorded the status of a separate peer group with their
own tribal rituals, customs and problems. They
were looked upon simply as children, to be seen and
not heard. Then New York became aware of an
unsettling phenomenon: thousands of screaming,
swooning girls had taken over the Paramount Theater.
Those who could not get in waited outside, in
bobbysocks and saddle shoes, hoping for a glimpse
of a then-obscure Pied Piper. He turned out to
be a skinny, jug-eared singer named Frank Sinatra.
Parents assumed that, like acne, he would go
away in time and that their children would return to
normal. They were wrong.

The Flashy Forties

In the 1940s, Broadway was host to memorable entertainment . . . *Oklahoma!* sent musicals into a new dimension. Ava Gardner was blossoming. Howard Lindsay and Dorothy Stickney graced *Life with Father*. Marquees carried names that survive: Betty Grable, Gregory Peck, Rita Hayworth, Kate Smith, Hedy Lamarr, Tyrone Power, Linda Christian. Marlon Brando, Jessica Tandy, Kim Hunter, Karl Malden won acclaim in *A Streetcar Named Desire*. Our favorite comedians were Bud Abbott and Lou Costello.

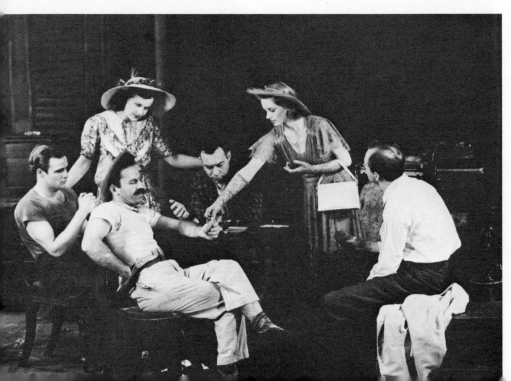

THE FIFTIES

"Let's talk sense to the American people. Let's tell them the truth, that there are no gains without pains."

Adlai Stevenson, 1952

Considered now by nostalgists to have been rather placid years, the Fifties were so only on the surface. Underneath was ferment and change.

The white supremacy of the South cracked as long-submerged blacks pushed their way up to what they called freedom. Whites in the cities pushed into the suburbs, leaving a vacuum that was to be filled by blacks moving North in pursuit of opportunity and equality. The U.S. Supreme Court ruled school segregation unconstitutional.

Politics sunk to a new low in the fraudulent Communist witch hunt conducted by glowering Senator Joseph McCarthy. The nation watched in fascination as the televised Kefauver hearings explored the corrupting network of organized crime in the cities.

The advent of the jet airplane changed American life and accelerated its tempo even more dramatically than did the progression from stagecoach to railroad a century and a half earlier. We became the most mobile people on earth.

We also became involved in a war in Korea. Perhaps it came too soon after World War II, but for whatever reason, only those touched personally by that war gave it much thought. The rest of us were preoccupied with adjusting to the post-World War II world.

The Caretaker Years

A resolutely apolitical President, Dwight D. Eisenhower, was in the White House. A sort of father-figure who made no waves, Eisenhower exercised his power paternally—easy-going generally, firm on occasion.

"The Last Great Hope"

The decade opened with bright hopes of peace and progress. The relationships among the United Nations in their East River showcase were reasonably amicable. The flags of the 76-member nations provided a colorful welcome to the thousands of tourists who came to see this "last great hope of mankind." But many New Yorkers wondered if there was any substance behind the glittering facade. There was. On June 25, 1950, 60,000 North Korean troops invaded South Korea. Two days later the UN Security Council voted military aid to the beleaguered South Koreans. We were plunged into a conflict whose toll was 33,629 killed, 103,284 wounded, yet which is scarcely more remembered than the Spanish-American War. The U.S. delegate to the UN was Warren Austin.

Cold War Casualties

Whipped to near-hysteria by leftist speakers, five thousand screaming,
weeping sympathizers protested the execution on June 19, 1953, of convicted
atom-spies Julius and Ethel Rosenberg. The Rosenbergs heard their
sentence impassively and died in Sing Sing's electric chair just as impassively.
Another controversial trial of the time saw Alger Hiss, one-time high
official of the State Department, convicted of perjury in denying that he had
passed secret documents to a then Communist courier, Whittaker Chambers.

FREEDOM BUS
TO
WASHINGTON, D.C.
OR
ANY OTHER CITY IN THE NORTH

Free Transportation plus $5.00 for Expenses to any Negro Man or Woman, or Family (no limit to size) who desire to migrate to the Nation's Capital, or any city in the north of their choosing. Please send your name and address to P.O. Box 899 New Orleans 2, La. You will be notified at an early date by the transportation company when you will leave.

On the back of this page you will find the names and addresses of the organizations who will help you when you arrive at any of the cities listed.

Listed here are the names, addresses, and telephone numbers of the organizations who will help you find jobs, houses, etc., when you arrive in any of these cities:

PITTSBURGH, PA.

NAACP	Urban League	Welfare Department
220 Grant Street	200 Ross Street	300 Liberty Avenue
Ph: GRant 1-1024	Ph: COurt 1-6010	Ph: EXpress 1-2100

CHICAGO, ILL.

NAACP	Urban League	Welfare Department
3856 S. South Park	2410 S. Michigan	100 W. Monroe St.
Ph: OA 4-5400	Ph: CA 5-0600	Ph: CE 6-4900

NEW YORK, N.Y.

NAACP	Urban League	Welfare Department
1722 Fulton Street	260 E. 161st St.	Borough Hall
Ph: HY 3-1671	Ph: CY 2-0596	336 Jay Street
		Ph: UL 5-3400

DETROIT, MICH.

NAACP	Urban League	Welfare Department
13122 Dexter St.	208 Mack Street	1010 Farmer
Ph: TO 9-6412	Ph: TE 2-4600	Ph: WO 3-1345

WASHINGTON, D.C.

NAACP	Urban League	Welfare Department
1417 U Street	626 3rd St.	330 Independence Ave
Ph: AD 2-2320	Ph: RE 7-0367	Ph: WO 3-1110

City of Refuge

Posters offering free transportation to the North were distributed in the South by segregationists. But blacks, by the hundreds of thousands, were already streaming into New York in search of a better life. A determined few found it; the rest found that they had exchanged one ghetto for another. Their frustrations were to boil over, with ominous results. Another tide of migration surged up from Puerto Rico. Ethnically aware, the Puerto Ricans followed the example of earlier immigrants and banded together to forge economic and political power. They parade their strength on New York's annual Puerto Rican Day.

White Flight

Another migration that was little noted until it was well underway was the exodus of whites to the suburbs, a massive population shift that changed the face of the city and confronted it with problems that remain unsolved. This is Levittown, Long Island, in 1950, one of the first of the mass-housing tracts.

Some Last Hurrahs

News then, forgotten now—still on the scene was the last of the old-time playboys, Tommy Manville, heir to the Johns-Manville asbestos fortune. A big spender who never tipped a waiter less than $50, Tommy was equally generous to his girl, or girls, of the moment. Not only that, he always did the honorable thing: he married them. Eleven of them. The ranking politicos of the Fifties were Abe Stark, Mayor Robert Wagner and Lawrence Gerosa. But the real political boss was Tammany chief Carmine DeSapio, whose tinted glasses lent him a faintly sinister air. Once, a cabdriver found a package containing $25,000 on the seat DeSapio had just vacated. The cabby turned it over to the police. The police called DeSapio. "What $25,000?" he asked.

So What's New?

Everything that happens in New York has happened before, including subway strikes. This one, in 1957, left the IND's cars sidetracked in the yards at 215th Street and Broadway while millions fumed. The only thing that grew in Brooklyn was a monstrous traffic jam along the Gowanus Parkway. The movie banner on the wall was offering *Search for Paradise,* but these hapless commuters were searching only for a way home.

No Longer the Only Way to Cross

The magnificent superliner *United States*—finest and fastest passenger ship ever built—proudly took her place in the Atlantic service in 1952 and quickly won the traditional Blue Ribband for her record crossing. But the day of the ocean queens was coming to an end. The agent of their demise—a new, jet-powered airplane called the Boeing 707—was already airborne. The 707 attracted a crowd of the curious when it arrived at the then Idlewild Airport for a series of tests.

Overleaf: In one of their last appearances together at the West Side piers were (top to bottom) the *Queen Mary*, *United States*, *America*, *Constitution* and *Cristoforo Colombo* (1958).

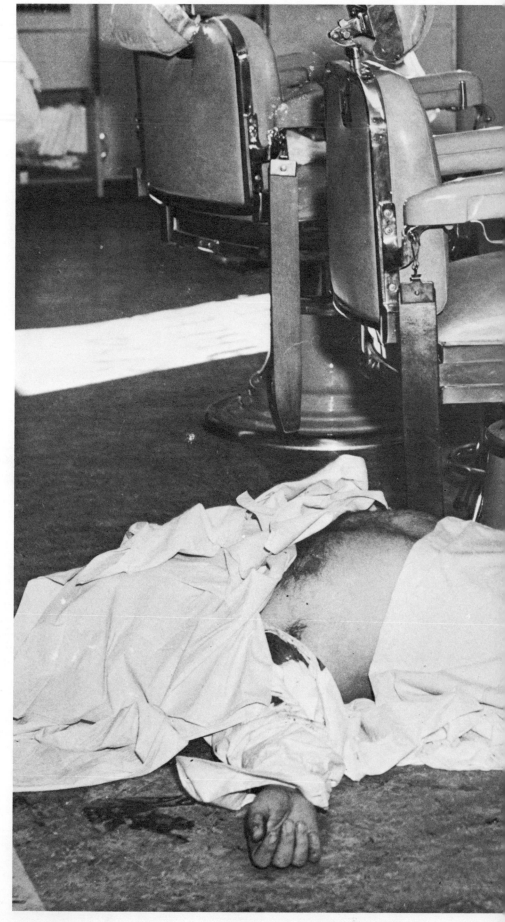

A Loser and a Loner

New Yorkers were becoming vaguely aware of an underworld alliance called the Mafia. It fixed itself in the public mind when one of its bosses, Albert Anastasia, died in a blaze of gunfire in the barbershop of the Park Sheraton Hotel in 1957. Peering wanly from behind bars in 1952 is another type of criminal, one who caught the public's fancy, an engaging scoundrel named Willie ("The Actor") Sutton. He masqueraded as a Western Union boy, postman, cop, flower deliveryman, even as Santa Claus, in a number of lone bank robberies. Asked once why a man of his intelligence and charm robbed banks, Willie forthrightly replied: "Because that's where the money is."

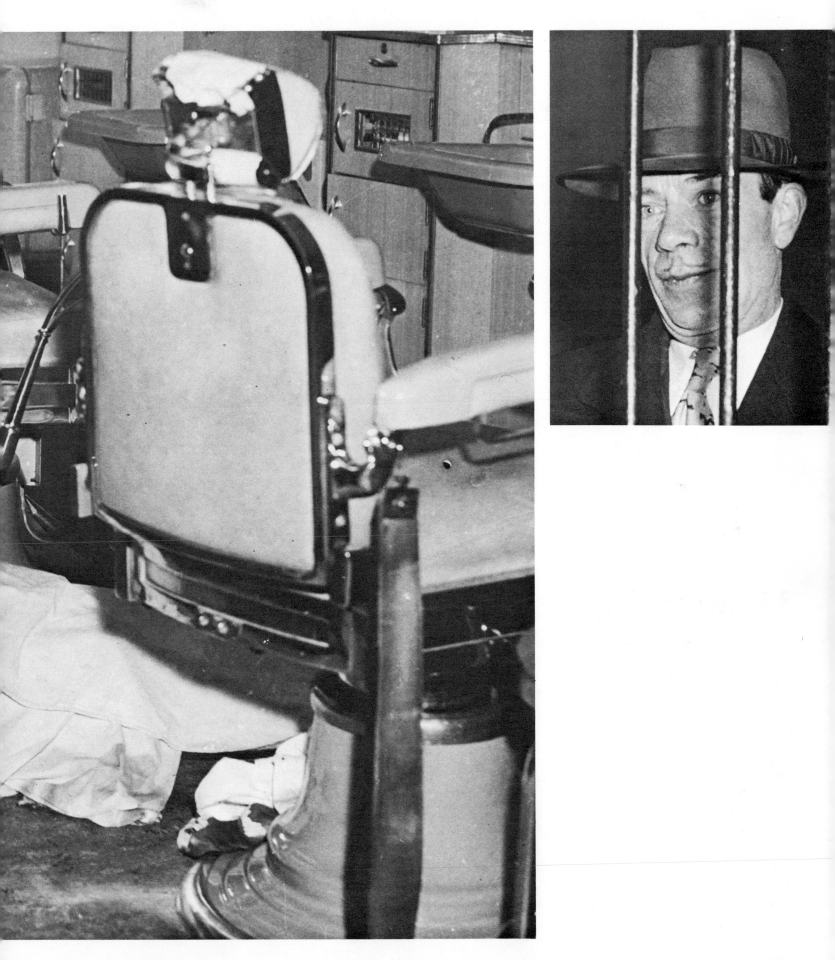

Taking a Subway to Salvation

Venturing out of the Bible Belt, the Rev. Billy Graham brought his crusade to New York, a city he thought would be a fertile field in which to harvest souls for the Lord. He was right. Times Square was jammed with seventy-five thousand followers at his farewell rally. Attractions like Billy Graham came and went, but the Roseland Ballroom was always there. In 1955 an exotic South American import called the mambo was all the rage.

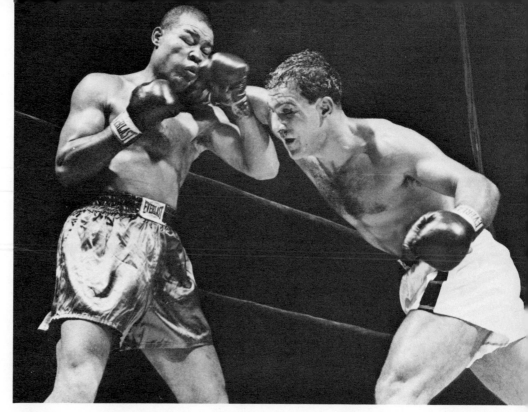

Headliners and a Headline

His skills eroded by time, former heavyweight champion
Joe Louis was battered into submission by the coming
champion, Rocky Marciano, at Madison Square Garden in
1951. In the last game of the 1956 season the Dodgers
won the pennant in what was then Brooklyn's most revered
"instatootion"— Ebbets Field. Then they vanished into
the smog of Los Angeles and Ebbets Field vanished soon
after. The Yankees had found a worthy successor to
Babe Ruth and Joe DiMaggio in a lead-miner's son from
Oklahoma—Mickey Mantle. A droll front page of
The Daily News recorded the impossible: the lowly
Dodgers had beaten the haughty Yankees in the 1955
World Series.

Memorable Moments

The man who broke the color line in baseball, Jackie Robinson, said goodbye to the Dodgers and the game after the 1956 season. The Fifties brought what is probably baseball's most dramatic moment: Bobby Thompson's ninth inning homer off Ralph Branca in the third game of the 1951 Giants-Dodgers playoff. It won the pennant for the Giants. One of the giants on the Giants was fabulous Willie Mays, who's making one of those circus catches that were routine for him.

Rock Rolls In

Led by gyrating Elvis ("The Pelvis") Presley, teenagers flocked to rock by the millions, embracing a new sound that two decades later still bombards the ear drums in today's discos. The goal of every New York kid was to get on Alan Freed's television show. One teenager who made it got fifteen hundred fan letters in a week.

Figures
of the Fifties

Although sex was an entirely private affair in that unpermissive decade, it had its public symbols: Jayne Mansfield could reflect from her exercise bar on the figure that took her from nameless New York photographer's model to a celebrity status that never quite reached stardom. A cabaret-circuit attraction, she was killed in an automobile accident while on tour in 1967. Even though Jane Russell and Marilyn Monroe were rivals in a sense (Marilyn's career overshadowed Jane's), they nonetheless graciously posed back to back for *The News* in 1953. Troubled and insecure despite her real talent as an actress, Marilyn died in 1962, possibly from an overdose of barbiturates.

Disasters

Flags fluttering, the Italian Lines' sleek, 30,000-ton *Andrea Doria* moved into lower New York Bay on her maiden voyage. Three years later, fatally holed in a collision with the Swedish-American Lines' *Stockholm* in 1956, she went to the bottom off Nantucket. Fifty-one lost their lives. Troubled then as now, the Long Island Rail Road took 110 people to their deaths in two catastrophic accidents in one year. On February 17, 1950, 31 were killed in Rockville Centre (top). On Thanksgiving Eve, November 22, 79 died in a telescoping collision in Richmond Hill, Queens.

Tube Talent

Television mesmerized us in the Fifties. The new medium made many new stars and widened the careers of established ones. Some show business luminaries of the decade: Milton Berle. Ed Sullivan. Jackie Gleason. Jimmy Durante. Elizabeth Taylor. Les Paul and Mary Ford. Burt Lancaster. Sophia Loren. Lucille Ball. Imogene Coca and Sid Caesar. Nat King Cole. Cary Grant. Gregory Peck. Fred MacMurray. The Rockettes were with us then as now.

THE SIXTIES

"That's one small step for a man, one giant leap for mankind."

—U.S. astronaut Neil A. Armstrong,
stepping onto the moon on July 20, 1969

The turbulent Sixties will more likely be remembered for their excesses than their achievements.

They were violent, bloody years. President John F. Kennedy, his brother Robert, and black leader Dr. Martin Luther King died at the hands of assassins. Black frustrations erupted in savage riots in the nation's cities, taking more than a hundred lives and destroying whole blocks.

College campuses seethed with rage and rebelliousness over the Vietnam War, a tragic conflict that came near to ripping the country apart and drove President Lyndon B. Johnson into retirement. Pessimists saw the turmoil as the dissolution of our society.

Yet there were notable achievements in those angry years. The voyage of Apollo 11 to the moon seems near-incredible even now. Progress in race relations sprung from the ruins of the ghettos; blacks found themselves for the first time in the mainstream of American life. The only revolution was in business, brought about by an electronic device called the computer.

He Died, His Dream Lives

"I had a dream . . ." The Rev. Martin Luther King, Jr., the most powerful
voice of his people in their struggles of the Sixties. Tragically he was to die at
the hands of an assassin only five years later.

Blessings and Blustering

New York was host to three important visitors in the Sixties. The most distinguished was Pope Paul VI, whose Mass for Peace at Yankee Stadium was attended by ninety thousand. The other two VIPs were Soviet Premier Nikita Khrushchev and Cuban Premier Fidel Castro, whose blustering was largely ignored by blasé New Yorkers. Unhampered by the diplomatic niceties, Khrushchev startled the staid UN General Assembly by taking off his shoe and pounding his desk with it during a speech that displeased him.

Spaced Out

Our first man to orbit the earth, John Glenn got a roaring welcome from the hundreds of thousands who massed on lower Broadway for his motorcade in 1962. Seven years later, the first moon men—Buzz Aldrin, Mike Collins and Neil Armstrong— drove through a blizzard of paper to accept the city's cheers for their magnificent achievement. *The News* and the other New York newspapers were out of orbit for 114 days because of a strike in 1963. The preoccupation of the lady below with the first post-strike paper indicates she missed the headlines.

Curtain Falls on Camelot

The assassination of President John F. Kennedy was a particularly stunning blow to New York, where he was tremendously popular. The city came to a standstill while television recorded the young President's funeral in Washington. Still another assassination bloodied a decade of senseless violence, that of Robert F. Kennedy, shown here at a Brooklyn rally with his brother's successor in the White House, President Lyndon B. Johnson.

Our Fair City

We had a World's Fair, our second. If you've forgotten, starting at the
left were the Philippines Pavilion, Greek Pavilion, African Nations complex,
Court of Nations, New Jersey's exhibit and the New York City Pavilion.
In the center is the Unisphere (1964). Governor Nelson Rockefeller was
The Boss in those years. Affable and breezy but with a whim of iron, he
ran the state and the Republican Party as if he owned both. Something new
in mayors moved into Gracie Mansion. John V. Lindsay was a Republican, an
Ivy Leaguer and very definitely not one of the masses. He and Mrs.
Lindsay were among the very first of what we now call the "in people."

A Dim View

The city had a blackout, its first. The view is from the News Building down Second Avenue, where only emergency lights burned. Gleaming like a diamond necklace against black velvet, the Verrazano Bridge remained alight, along with parts of Staten Island and Brooklyn (1965).

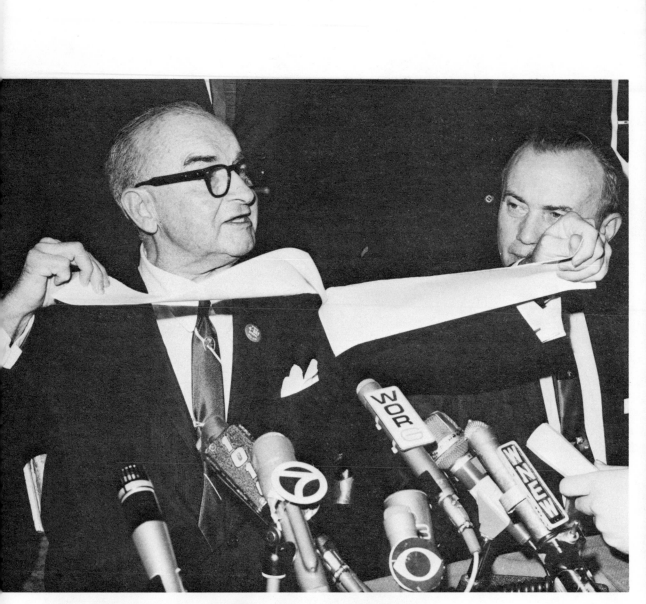

The Day the Subways Stopped

The then chief of the Transit Workers Union, Mike Quill, tore up a temporary strike-barring injunction only minutes after Lindsay became the 103rd Mayor of New York in 1966. The only things that moved in the subways were the thumbs twiddled by an occasional policeman. This one stood guard in the Grand Central Station of the IRT Flushing Line. The empty train was parked there for safekeeping. Quill (in the light hat) was hustled off to jail for ignoring the court order. Stricken there with a heart attack, he was to die later. The strike went on.

Overleaf: Manhattan beckoned from across the East River, but you couldn't get there from Brooklyn, where the strike-bound buses were parked. Traffic became a nightmare dreamed by Franz Kafka. Quite a few motorists, totally defeated, abandoned their cars in the middle of the street and walked away into a night of blaring horns. This was Third Avenue, looking south from 42nd Street. The strike was settled after twelve days, but at a cost that New York would have to reckon with in later years.

Riotous Times

There were riots for all seasons and reasons. This one erupted on the East Side one muggy night over nothing but a fist fight. Fire bombs were thrown, a dozen people hurt, two arrested. Flag burnings were a fairly common occurrence. This one was the work of something called "Spring Mobilization Against the War in Vietnam." It took place in Central Park's Sheep Meadow, attended by 125,000 protestors and 3,000 police.

Hail Columbia!

Columbia University was a particular target. Fiery activist Mark Rudd (in plaid shirt), dimly remembered today, led rebellious students in a fierce but relatively bloodless charge against campus guards. With the crash-ins and sit-ins at Columbia went mindless juvenile vandalism, called trashing. This was the scene in the office of Columbia vice president David Truman after sit-in demonstrators were thrown out. Not to be outdone, welfare workers and their customers clashed with police in a wild melee at 42nd Street and Lexington Avenue. Nobody ever knew why.

Erasing a Landmark

The city suffered some architectural wrenches, too. The dowager queen of mid-Manhattan, Grand Central Station, found herself overwhelmed by the looming bulk of the Pan-Am Building. That stately pile, Pennsylvania Station, an awe-inspiring sight to visiting outlanders in the early years of the century, was ticketed for the wrecker's ball. At least its 14 majestic, 5,700-pound granite eagles were saved from routine destruction.

Beautiful Bridgework

The decade saw at least one jewel added to the city's crown—the magnificent sweep of the Verrazano Bridge, whose 4,200 feet make it the world's longest suspension span. Staten Island is on the left, Brooklyn on the right, Manhattan in the background. But old Penn Station disappeared altogether, replaced by today's Madison Square Garden complex.

Going Like Sixty

In sports, the Sixties brought championship seasons to the Mets, the Jets and the Knicks. Knicks fans still cherish the memories of that fabulous 1969–70 season when, with superstar Willis Reed soaring toward the basket like Superman, their heroes won it all. But not even the skills of Rod Gilbert, shown here as he scored a goal against Philadelphia, could help the hapless Rangers.

Broadway Joe

New York's undisputed king of sports was jet-setter Broadway Joe Namath, who quarterbacked the Jets to the Super Bowl in 1969–70 and delighted his fans by coolly promising, and just as coolly delivering, a victory over Baltimore. He might have come from Beaver Falls, Pennsylvania, but Joe took to New York as it took to him. His fan mail ran one hundred letters a day, almost all of it from girls. If you're a New Yorker, you know what this mob scene is. If you're not, well, it's The Day the Mets Won the World Series in 1969. It was pandemonium at Shea Stadium.

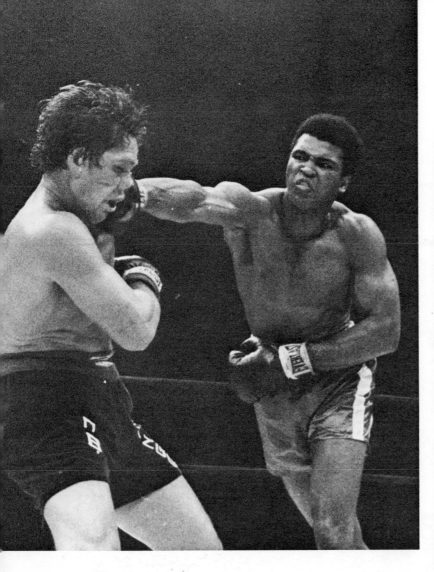

Belting It Out

Muhammad Ali did it with muscle and the Beatles did it
with music. Ali packed Madison Square Garden in all
of his New York fights. In this particular bout, Oscar
Bonavena happened to be on the receiving end of a hard
right, but in the Sixties it didn't really matter who
Ali's opponent was: they all went down. It was bedlam
at the ball park, Beatlemania, when a turnaway
crowd of shrieking teenagers strained the capacity of
Shea Stadium to see, and possibly even hear, their
idols, the Beatles. Scores were injured in the crush.

Meeting of the Mindless

The Sixties were the time of hippies, yippies and flower children, all determined to defy The Establishment by doing their thing, no matter how idiotic. One group invaded the New York Stock Exchange where, to show their disdain for money, they burned a few bills before the annoyed capitalists threw them out. The scruffy avant-garde took itself with solemn seriousness. Even its garb was symbolical, although the symbolism of the gas mask was and is obscure. In what was billed as a "put-down of middle-class values," a band of East Village hippies embarked on a bus tour of Queens, stopping en route to stage a naked flesh-in at a place in Hillside called the Nirvana Headshop. Hillside was not amused, but neither was it shocked. It all seems rather foolish now.

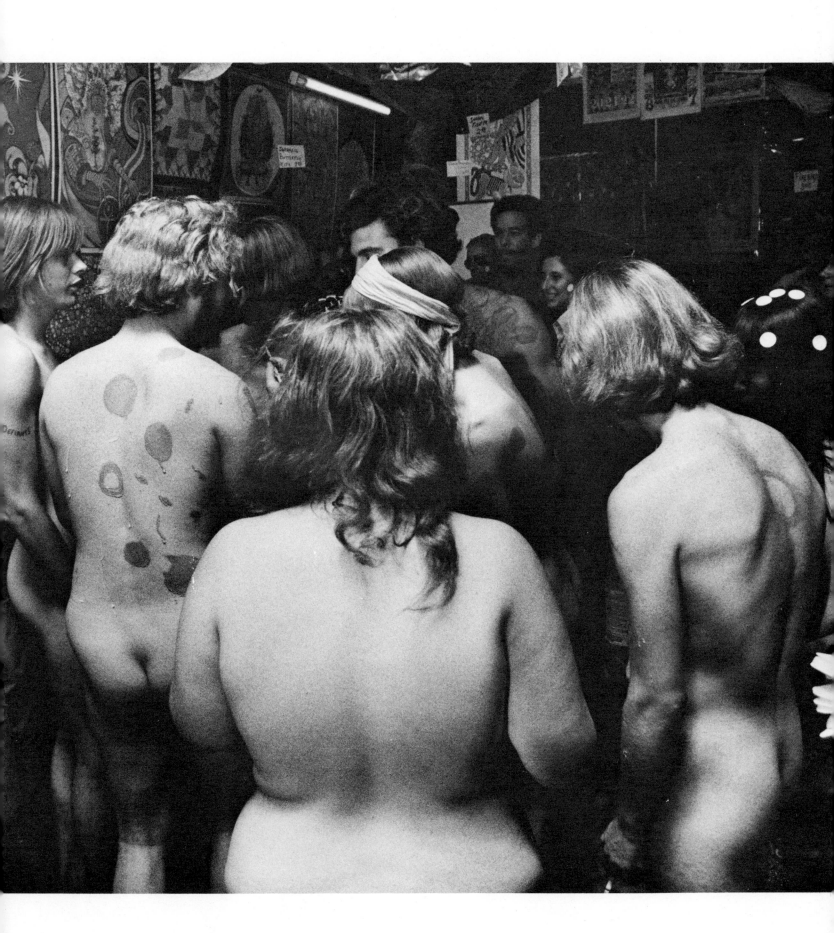

Decibels and Derrieres

The disco, with its impromptu, frenetic dancing, entered the New York scene. The odd behavior of the two men at the table was unexplained. Were they overcome by the ambiance or were they ducking the photographer? Fashion underwent some changes, too. The miniskirt came into style and produced only two reactions. Model Anita Ervin drew both from the man and woman she passed on Third Avenue. Then came hot pants.

O, Jackie!

The most-photographed New York celebrity of the Sixties and Seventies, Jacqueline Kennedy Onassis was and is pursued by lensmen night and day. Jim Hughes caught her and husband Aristotle Onassis as they left an East Side restaurant. A smiling Jackie emerged from a limousine outside her Fifth Avenue apartment. She had just returned from a vacation on Onassis' private Greek island, Skorpios. An angry Jackie sent *News* photographer Mel Finkelstein sprawling when he took her picture on West 57th Street. "I had just finished shooting her picture," said Finkelstein, "when she came toward me, grabbed my right arm, put her left leg out and flipped me over."

Roger Who?

Roger Maris, that's who. He broke Babe Ruth's one-season, home-run record but is remembered today only as a statistic. Others in the public eye in the Sixties remain fresh in the memory: (from bottom, left to right) Ann-Margret. Gina Lollobrigida. Rock Hudson. (opposite page, left to right by rows) Tammy Grimes. Jack Lemmon. Eva Marie Saint. Robert Stack. Dina Merrill. Robert Redford. Shirley MacLaine. George Peppard. Leslie Caron.

urning Off the Limelight

he Sixties in New York were Mayor John V. Lindsay's era, and the era
eally did not end until January 1, 1974, when he switched off the last lamp
t Gracie Mansion and walked out of New York political life.

Photo Credits: 60 (bottom left) Detroit Mirror Photo; 64-65 Fairchild Photo;
86 (bottom) Joe Costa; 88 (bottom) Ossie Leviness; 106 (top) Martin McEvilly;
108 (top) Charles Hoff; 109 Charles Hoff; 120 (top) Joe Costa; 142-143
Paul Bernius; 144, 145 Seymour Wally; 152 George Mattson; 153 (top) Bob Koller,
(bottom) Bill Wallace; 154 Harold Mathewson; 155 (top) George Torrie,
(bottom) Walter Kelleher; 157 Bob Koller; 160 (bottom) Harold Mathewson;
162 John Duprey; 163 (top) Ed Peters, (bottom) George Mattson; 165 Ed Giorandino;
166-167 Gordon Rynders; 168 Tom Baffer; 169 Ebbs Breuer; 170 (top) Al Pucci,
(bottom) David McLane; 171 Bill Quinn; 172 (top) Charles Hoff; 173 (cartoon)
Leo O'Mealia, (right) Charles Hoff; 174 (top) Charles Payne, (bottom) George Torrie;
175 Charles Hoff; 178 Harold Mathewson; 180 (top) Bill Meurer, (bottom)
Gordon Rynders and Ed Clarity; 181 (top) Bill Meurer, (bottom) Tom Gallagher;
185, 186 Frank Hurley; 187 (top) John Duprey, (bottom) Frank Hurley; 188
(top) Paul Bernius, (bottom) Seymour Wally; 189 Dan Farrell; 190, 191 Dan Farrell;
192 Gordon Rynders; 193 (top) Harold Mathewson, (bottom) Dan Farrell;
194-195 Gordon Rynders; 196 Paul DeMaria; 197 (top) Ed Clarity, (bottom)
Judd Mehlman; 198 Bob Koller; 199 Bill Quinn; 200 Jim Mooney; 201, 202
(top) Leonard Detrick; 202 (bottom), 203 Jim Garrett; 204 John Duprey; 205
(bottom) Ed Giorandino; 206 Harry Hamburg; 207 Gordon Rynders; 208
Dan Farrell; 209 Frank Hurley; 210 Dan Farrell; 211 (top) Mel Finkelstein, (bottom)
Dan Farrell; 212, 213 Dan Farrell; 214 (top) Jack Smith, (bottom) Judd Mehlman;
215 Anthony Casale; 216 (top) Dennis Caruso, (bottom) Judd Mehlman; 217
Dennis Caruso; 218 (top) Jim Hughes; 218 (bottom), 219 Anthony Casale; 223
Richard Corkery

Design: Irwin Glusker
Layout assistants: Cela Wright, Phil Abrams
Composition: Compo-Set Typographers, Inc.
Printing and binding: A. Horowitz & Sons, Fairfield, N.J.